MY FIRST BOOK OF
DOT MARKER
COLORING

Woo! Jr. Kids Activities Founder: Wendy Piersall

Book Layout by: Michael Koch
Cover Illustration: Michael Koch

Published by DragonFruit, an imprint of Mango Publishing, a division of Mango Publishing Group, Inc.

For permission requests, please contact the publisher at:

Mango Publishing Group
2850 Douglas Road, 2nd Floor
Coral Gables, FL 33134 USA
info@mango.bz

For special orders, quantity sales, course adoptions and corporate sales, please email the publisher at sales@mango.bz. For trade and wholesale sales, please contact Ingram Publisher Services at customer.service@ingramcontent.com or +1.800.509.4887.

My First Book of Dot Marker Coloring

ISBN: 978-1-64250-713-3

BISAC: JNF001010, JUVENILE NONFICTION / Activity Books / Coloring

Dot Marker Coloring!

Are you ready to color with MARKERS?

Dot marker coloring is easy to learn! All you have to do is take the marker you want and fill in the white dots or circles.

Look at how this parrot has a bunch of different fun colors in his dots!

On the next page there's a half-finished Teddy Bear that needs a few more dots filled!

Grab the color that matches the most and help finish the picture!

P.S. It's ok if your markers don't match every color on the page perfectly. Choose whichever color you like and have **FUN!**

Practice Here!

Can you
finish coloring the
Scene?

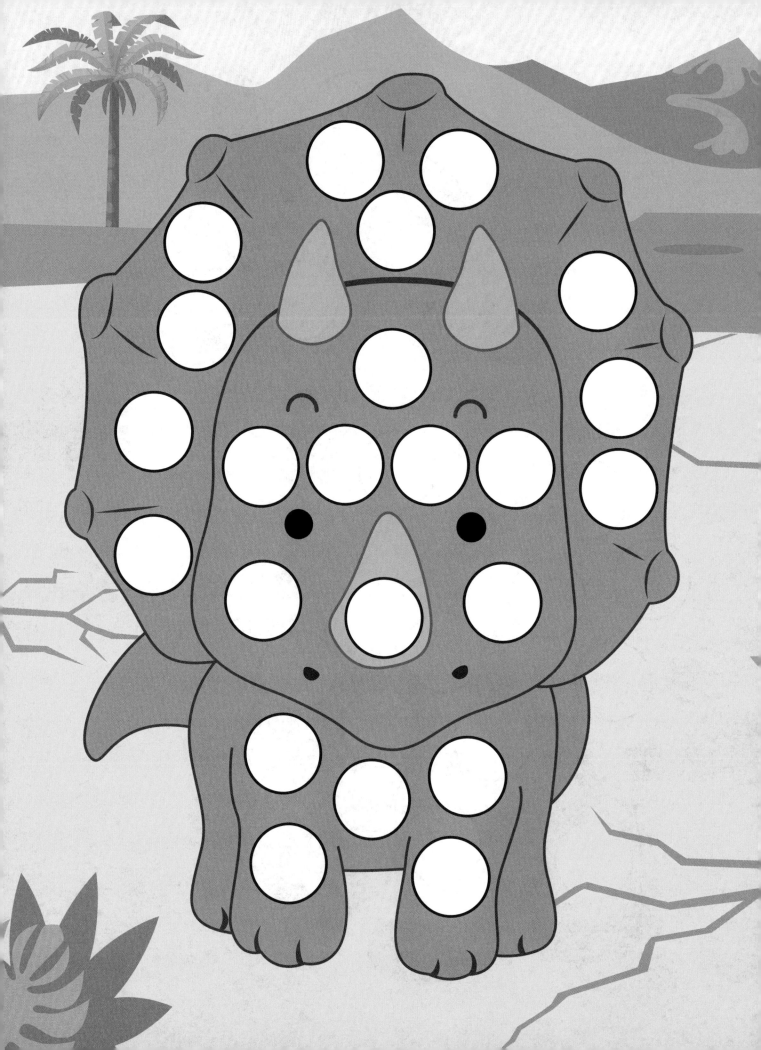

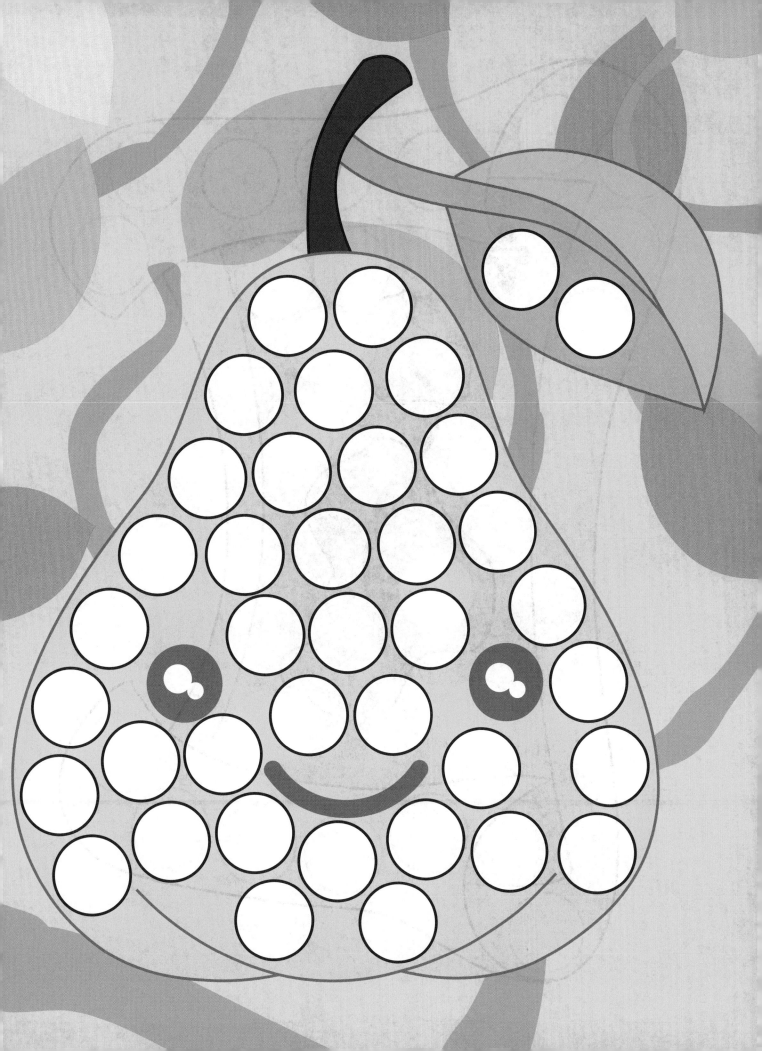

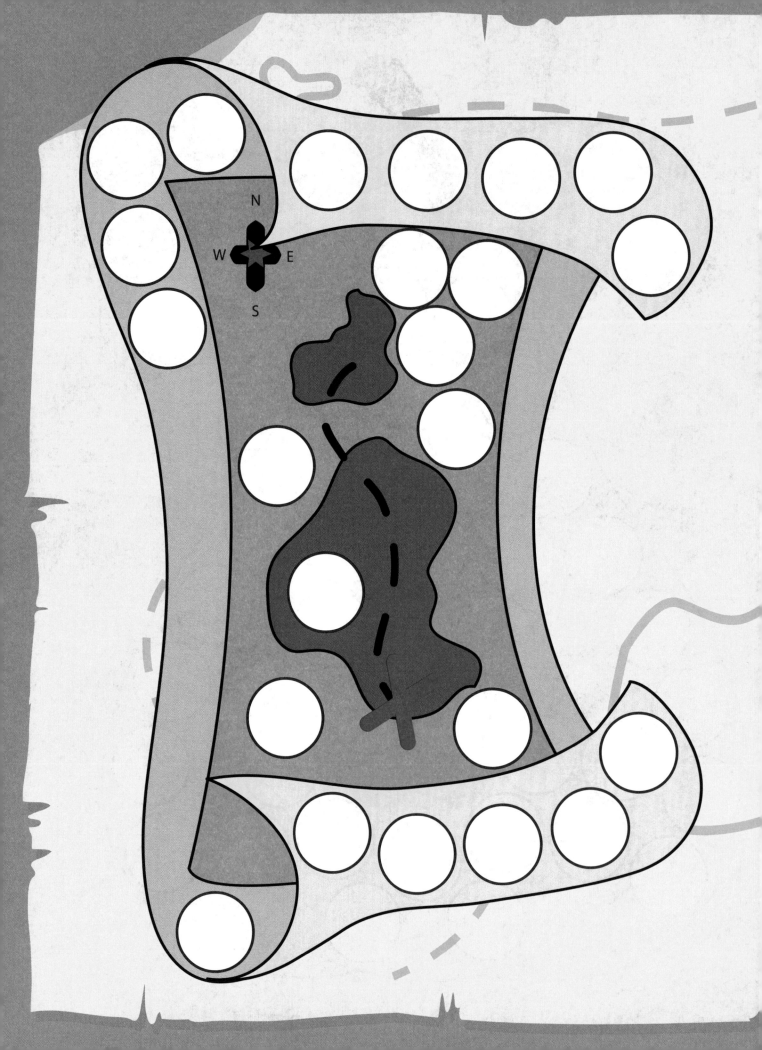

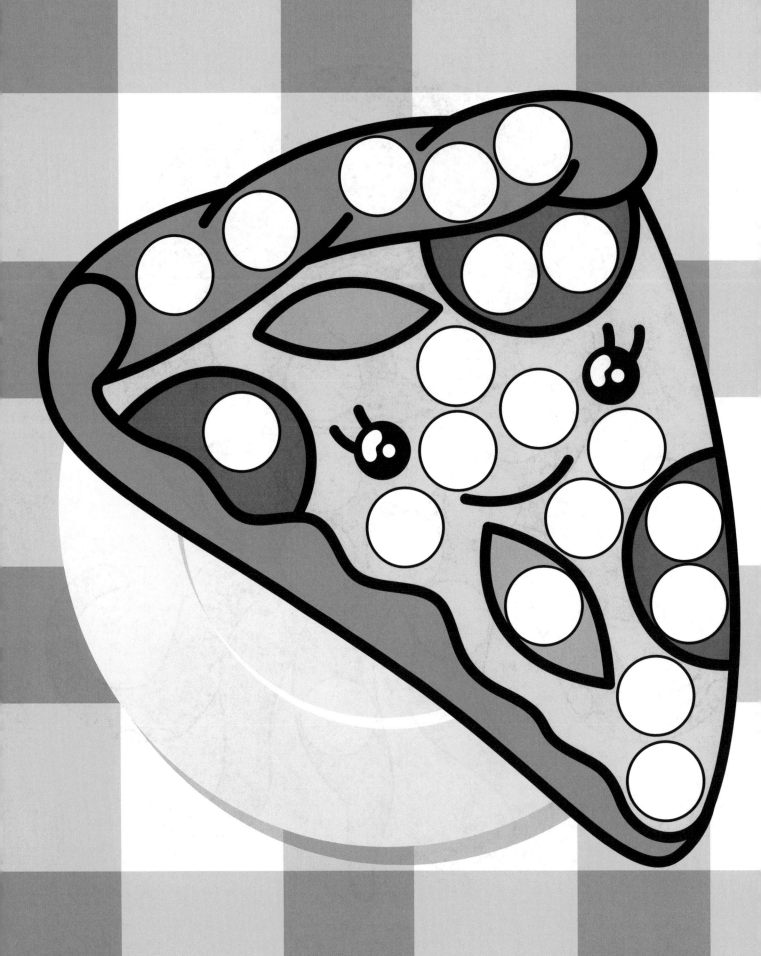

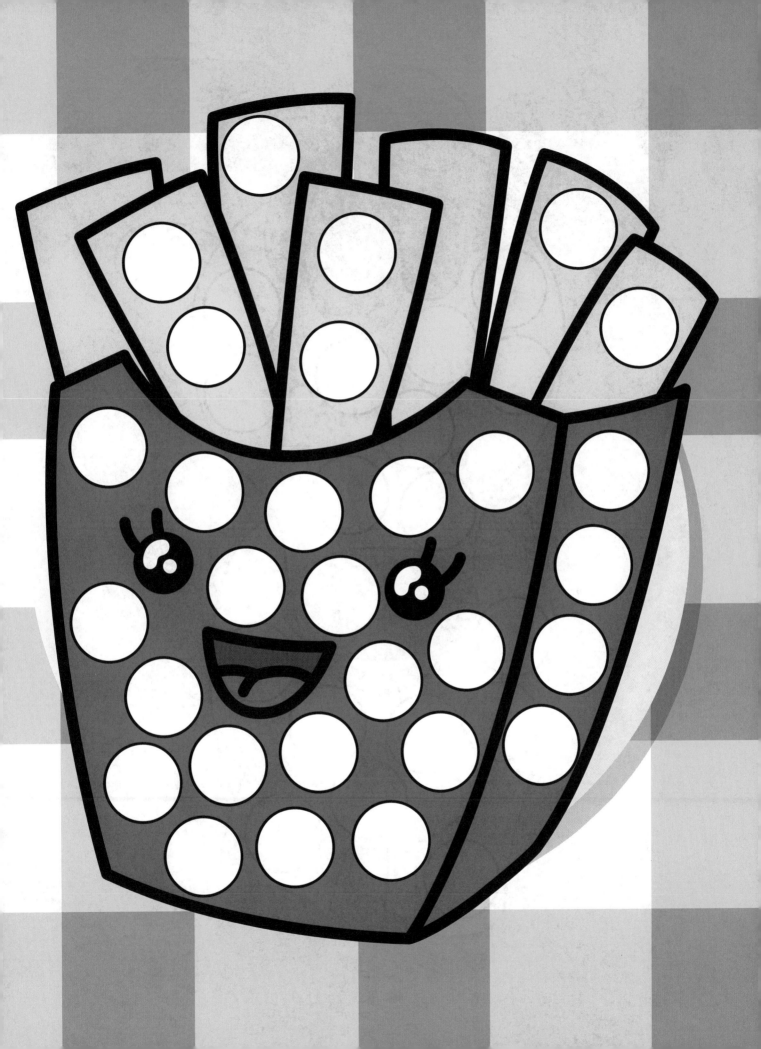

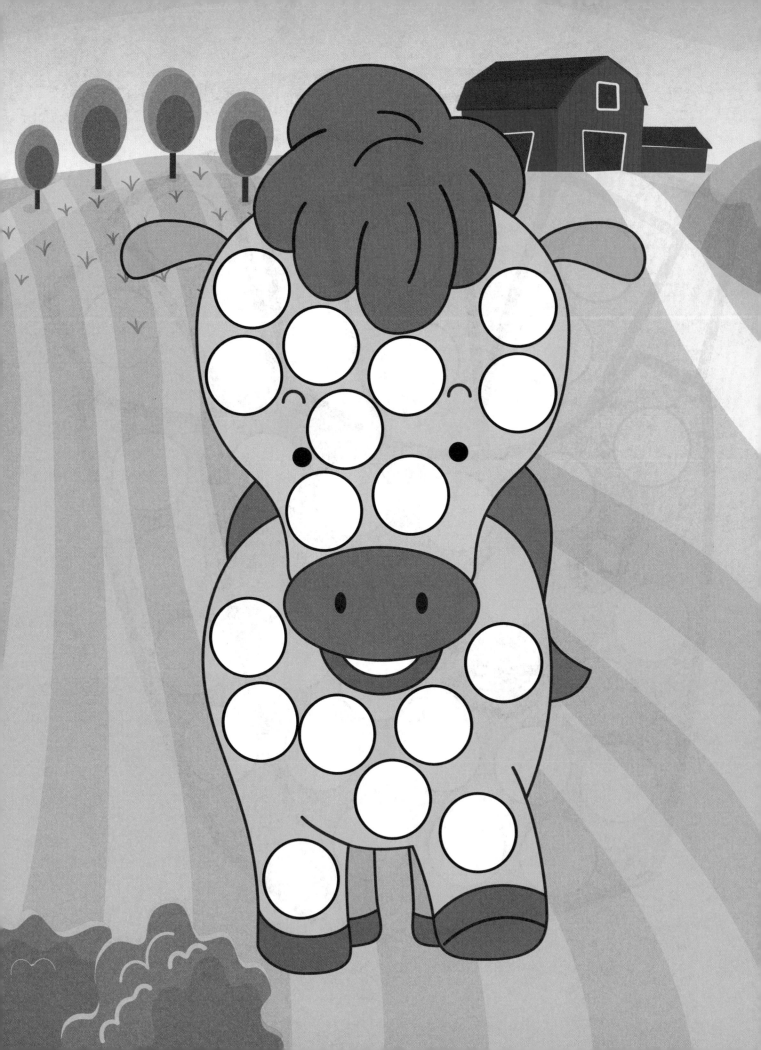

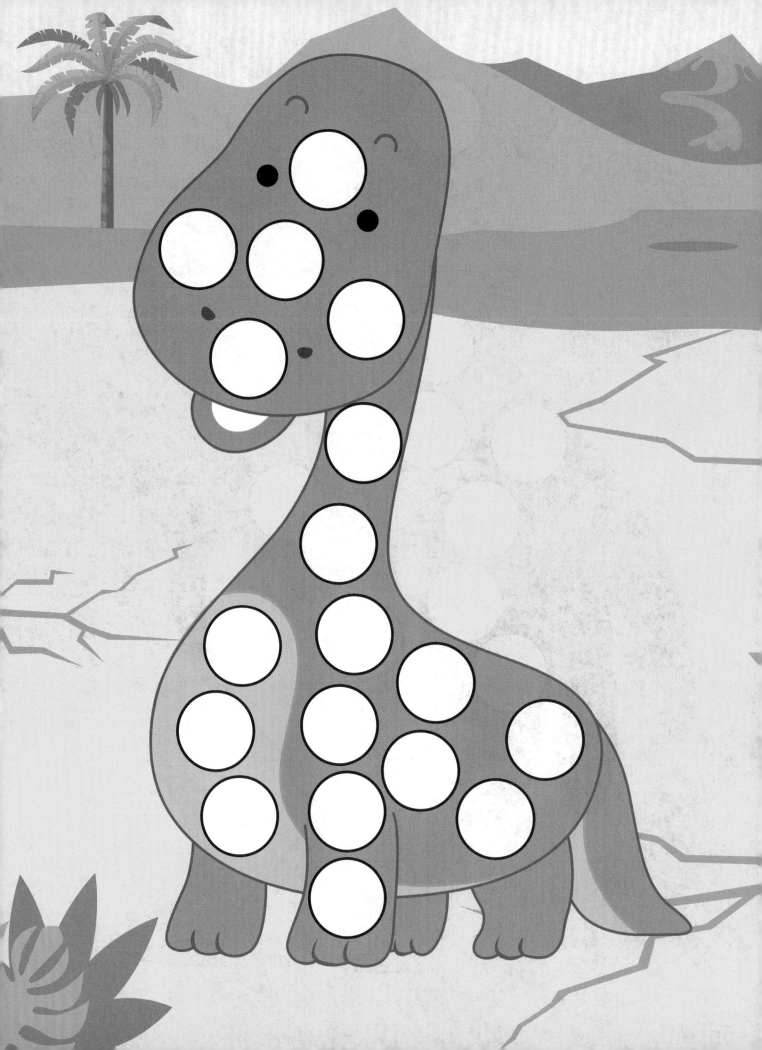

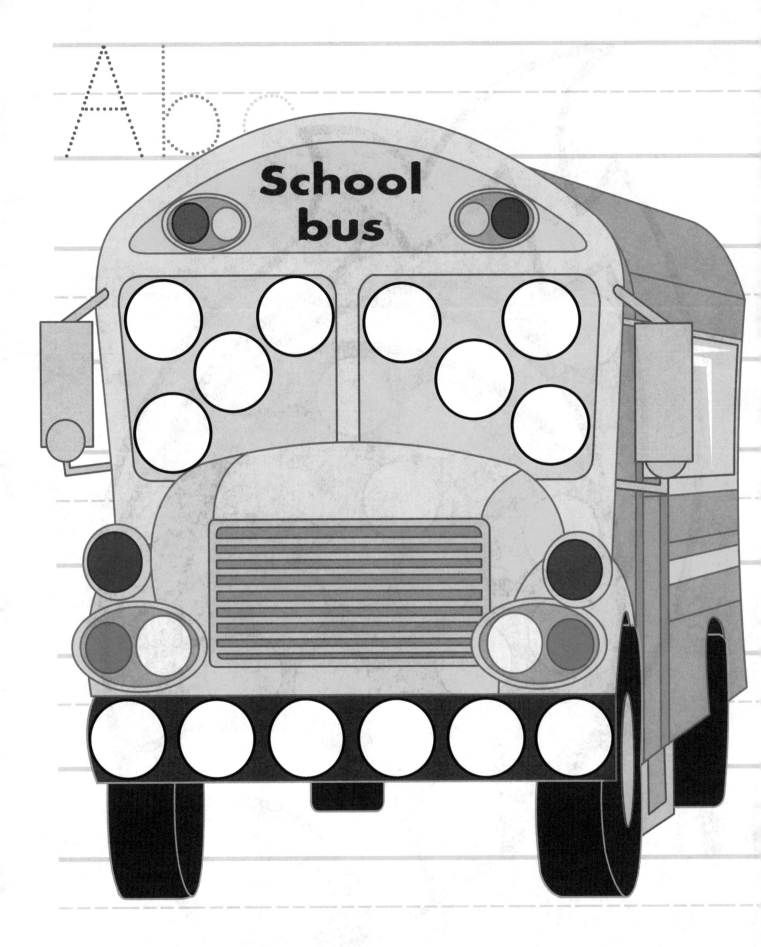

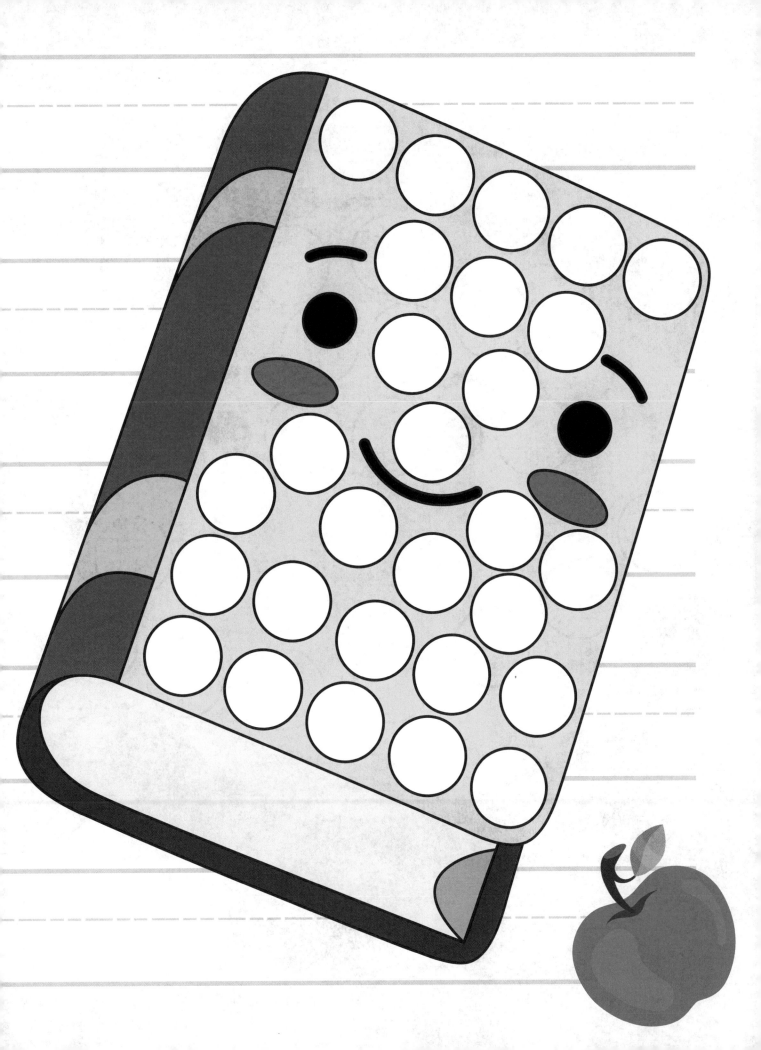

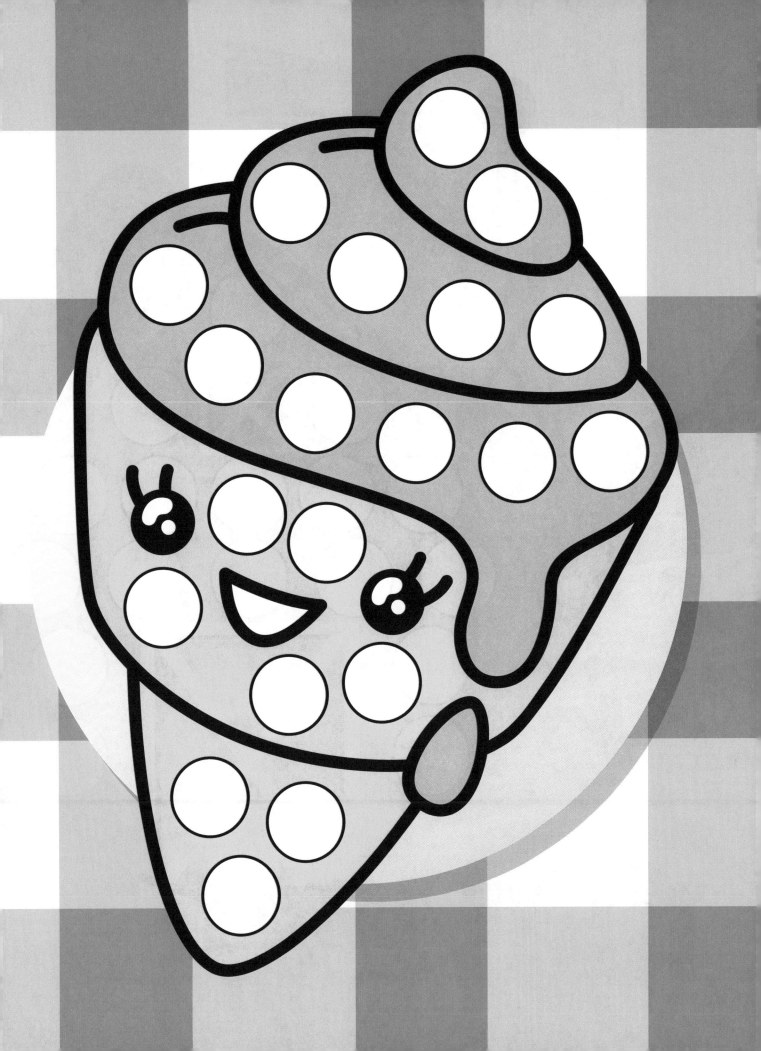

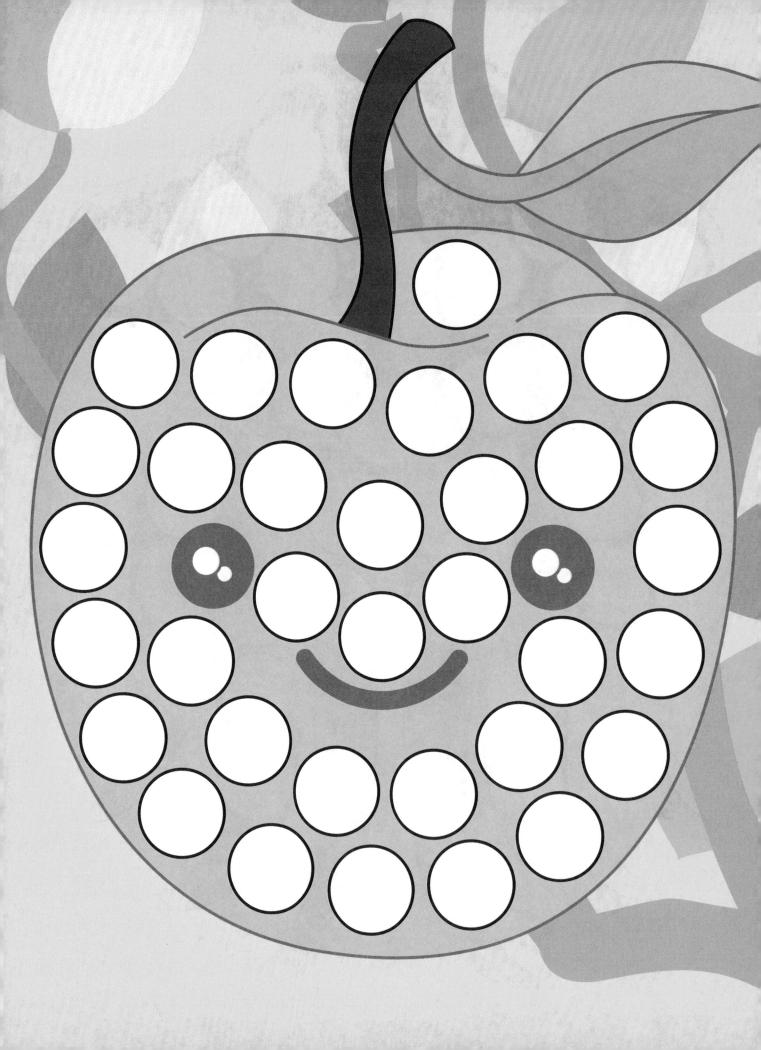

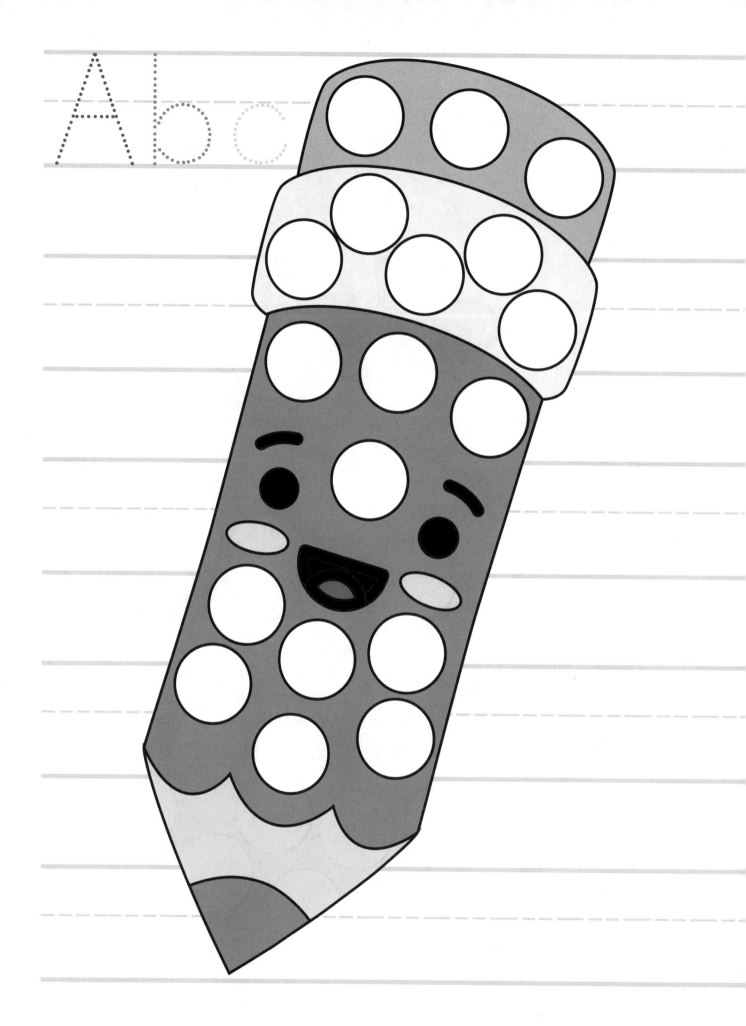

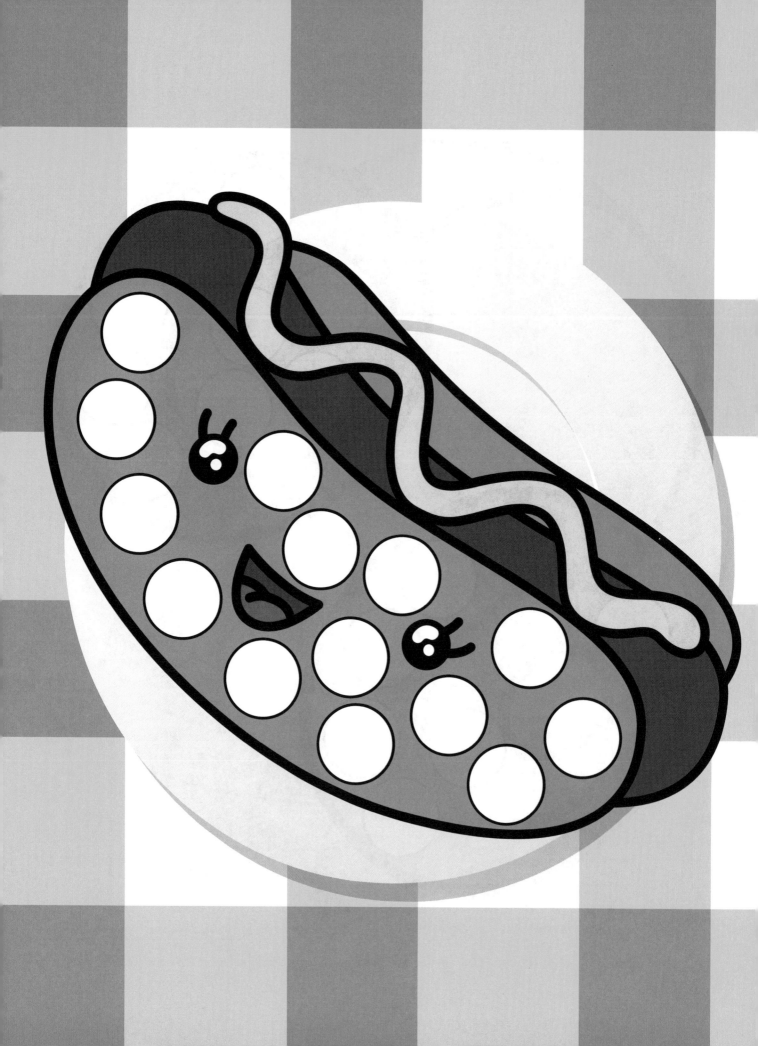

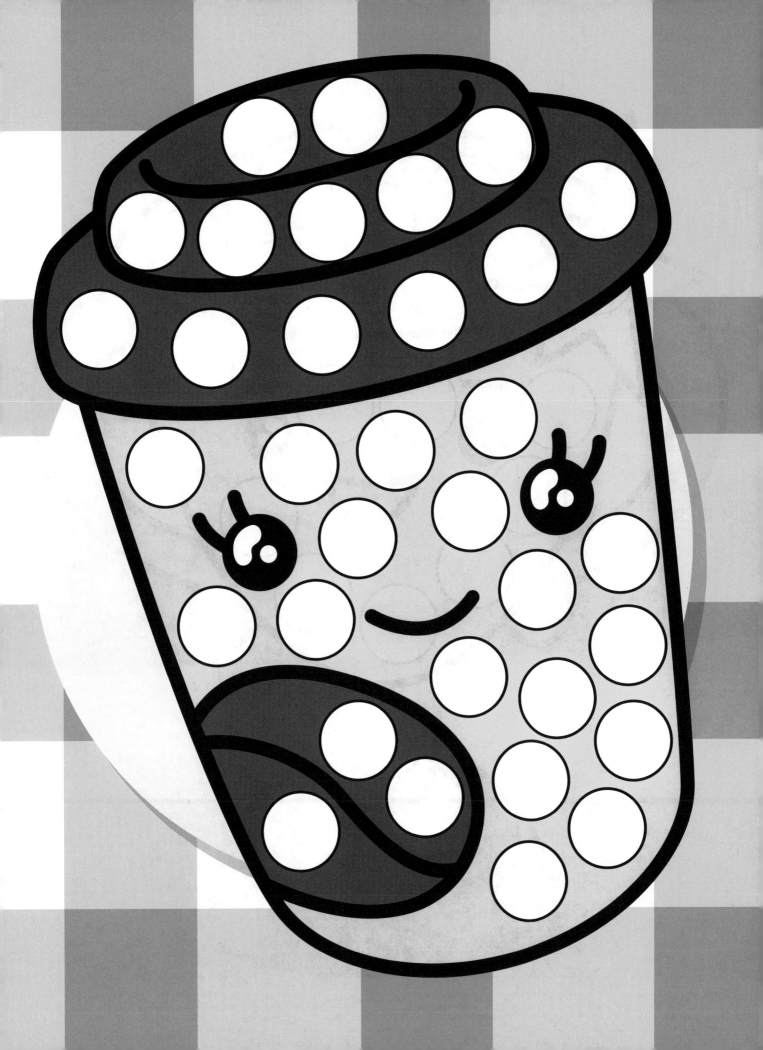

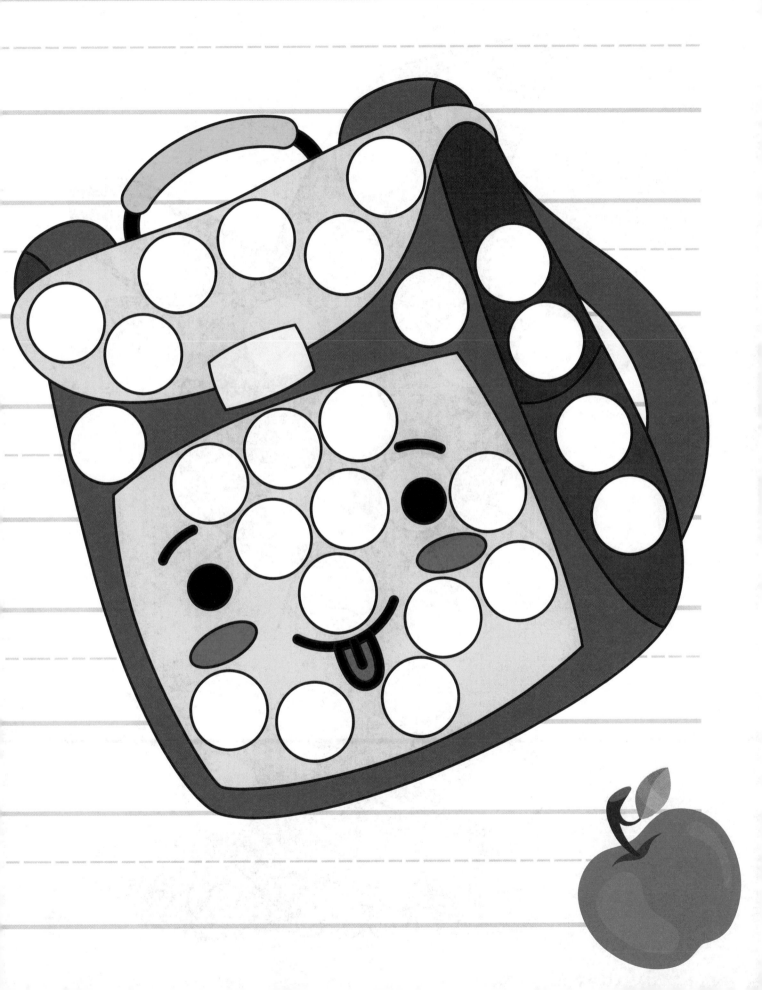

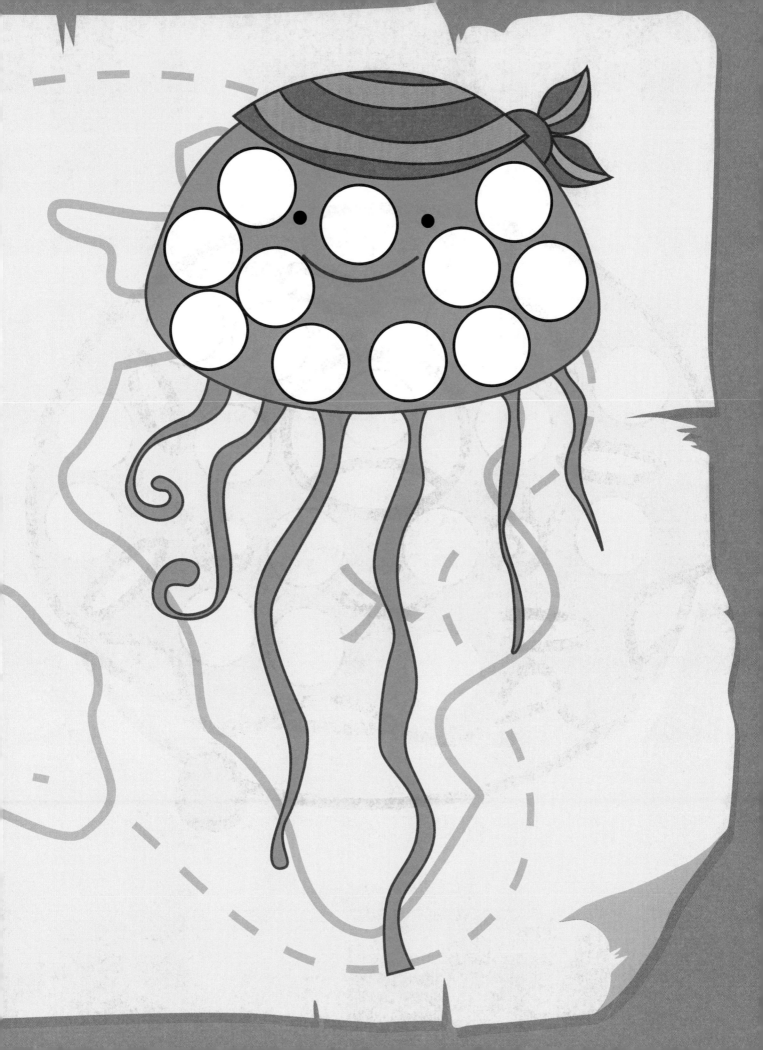

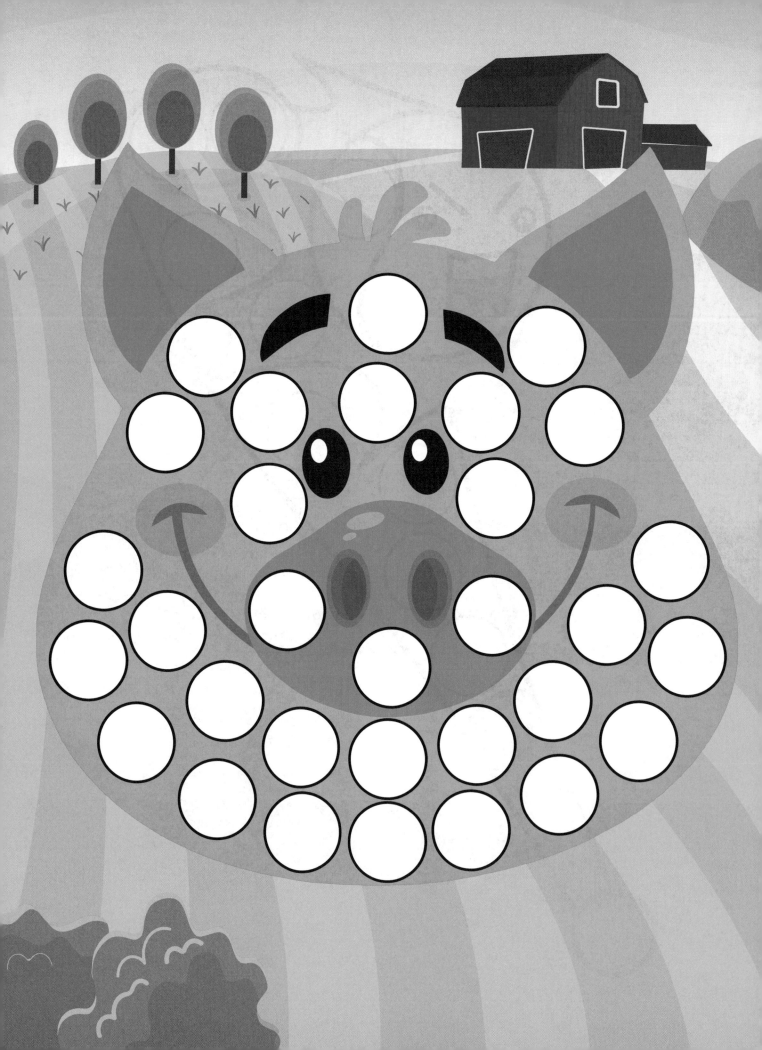

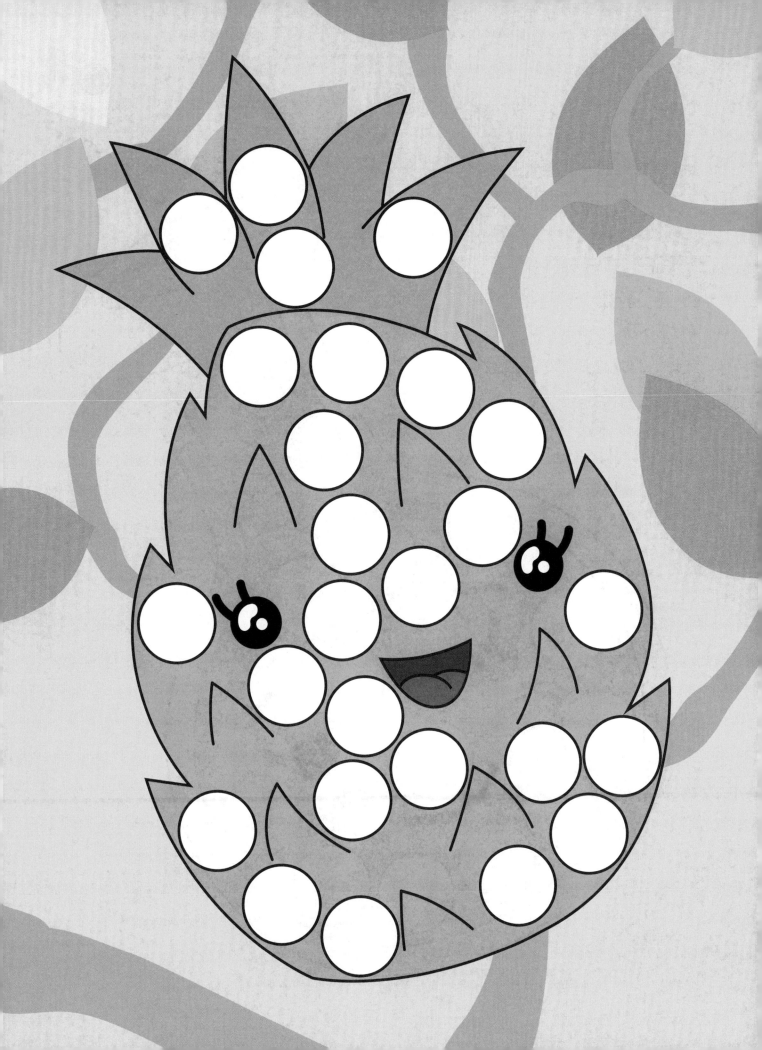

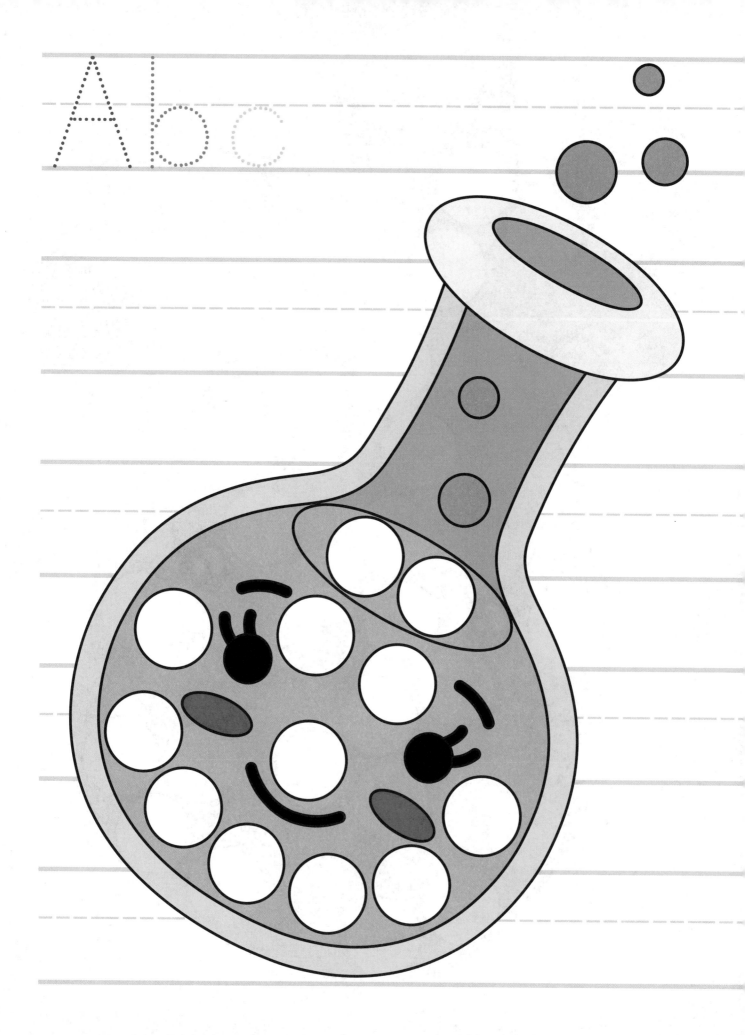

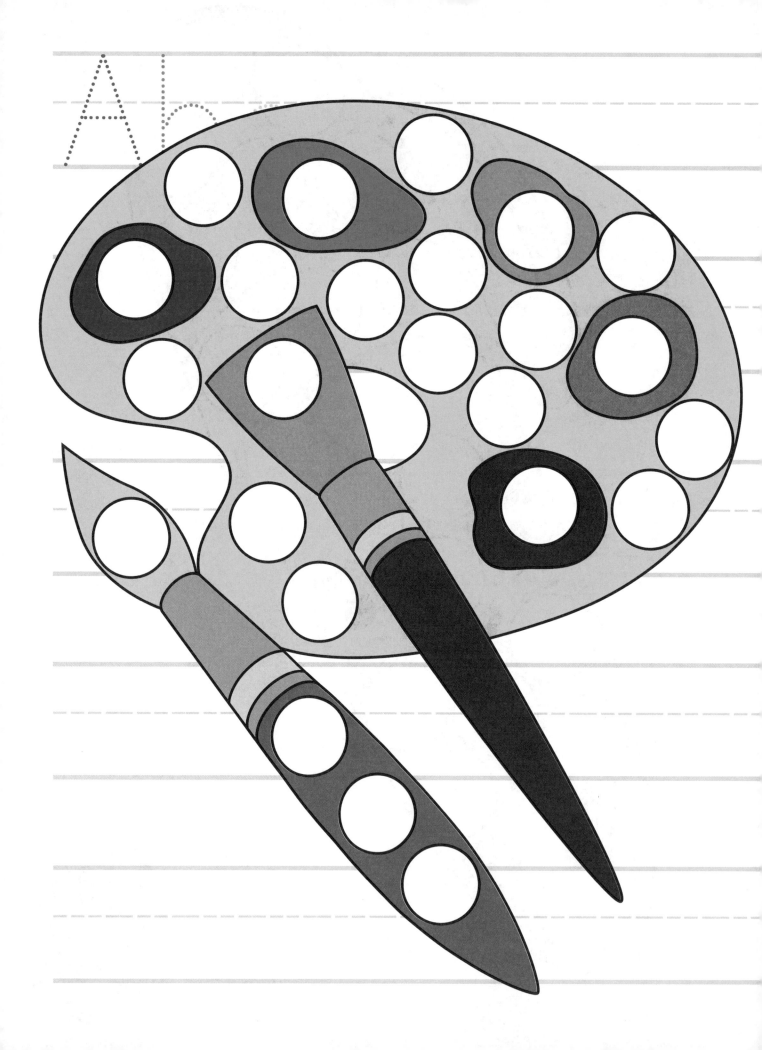

Woo! Jr. Kids Activities is passionate about inspiring children to learn through imagination and FUN. That is why we have provided thousands of craft ideas, printables, and teacher resources to over 55 million people since 2008. We are on a mission to produce books that allow kids to build knowledge, express their talent, and grow into creative, compassionate human beings. Elementary education teachers, day care professionals, and parents have come to rely on Woo! Jr. for high-quality, engaging, and innovative content that children LOVE. Our bestselling kids activity books have sold over 375,000 copies worldwide.

Tap into our free kids activity ideas at our website WooJr.com or by following us on social media:

https://www.pinterest.com/woojrkids/
https://www.facebook.com/WooJr/
https://twitter.com/woojrkids
https://www.instagram.com/woojrkids/

DragonFruit, an imprint of Mango Publishing, publishes high-quality children's books to inspire a love of lifelong learning in readers. DragonFruit publishes a variety of titles for kids, including children's picture books, nonfiction series, toddler activity books, pre-K activity books, science and education titles, and ABC books. Beautiful and engaging, our books celebrate diversity, spark curiosity, and capture the imaginations of parents and children alike.

Mango Publishing, established in 2014, publishes an eclectic list of books by diverse authors. We were named the Fastest-Growing Independent Publisher by Publishers Weekly in 2019 and 2020. Our success is bolstered by our main goal, which is to publish high-quality books that will make a positive impact in people's lives.

Our readers are our most important resource; we value your input, suggestions, and ideas. We'd love to hear from you—after all, we are publishing books for you!

Please stay in touch with us and follow us at:

Instagram: @dragonfruitkids

Facebook: Mango Publishing

Twitter: @MangoPublishing

LinkedIn: Mango Publishing

Pinterest: Mango Publishing

Sign up for our newsletter at www.mangopublishinggroup.com and receive a free book! Join us on Mango's journey to change publishing, one book at a time.

Of WOMB *and* TOMB